A Bit About LIFE

A COLLECTION OF SHORT POEMS ABOUT
LIFE, LOVE & DEATH AND EVERYTHING IN BETWEEN

S.N. SIPPY

Published in 2023
By S.N. SIPPY

© S.N. SIPPY 2023
snsippy@hotmail.com

ISBN: 978-1-913898-44-1

Book Production by Russell Holden
www.pixeltweakspublications.com

Dedicated to the memory of my
dear Mother who was and has
continued to have a meaningful
influence on my life.

She was a wise woman
and a loving Mother.

CONTENTS

The poems that you are about to read have emerged straight from my heart based on an experience of a lifetime.

I have also been greatly influenced by the teachings in the Bhagavat Gita.

As with life, some of these poems are dark in nature whilst others are full of hope and opportunity.

Putting pen to paper has been a cathartic experience for me and here's hoping that these poems will inspire you and bring you solace and the strength to carry on through the ups & downs that most of us must face in our daily lives.

A Bit About Life

Why is Life so complicated?
Analysing life makes it complicated, stop analysing, just live it

Why are we constantly unhappy?
Worrying makes us unhappy

How can we not worry when there is so much uncertainty?
Uncertainty is inevitable, worrying is optional

There is so much pain
Pain is inevitable, suffering is optional

In tough times, how to stay motivated?
Always look how far you have come
rather than how far you have to go.
Count your blessings, not your losses

How to get the best out of life
Face your past without regret, handle your present with confidence, prepare for the future without fear

The enhancement of mental and inner strength comes from struggle and endurance, not when you are free from problems.

Keep your faith and drop your fear, don't believe your doubts, and doubt your beliefs.
Have a happy life.

BE THE EAGLE

May you soar over clouds where eagles dare

May you rise above good and evil

Happiness and sadness

May your efforts be their own reward

May you be wise beyond your years

Can You?

Can you think when you want to think
And stop when you don't?
Can you use your imagination at will?
Can you accept without regret
And adapt to change?
Can you give without remembering
And receive without forgetting?
Can you find joy in simple things
And not be easily impressed?
Can you be content with what you have
But not give up on your ambitions?
Can you enjoy the company of friends
But enjoy solitude as well?
Can you connect with people
But not be too attached?
Can you as a grown-up
Carry the curiosity of a child?
Can you seize the gap between your thoughts
And widen this with intent
To delve into pure consciousness?
Can you?
If you can, you will hold the world in the palm of
your hand.

COMPARISON

If you must compare yourself
Then compare yourself with yourself
With yourself as you were yesterday
And check for progress within yourself.

Comparison with others is futile
Chase your own dreams
To become your own self
For that is truly the best place to be.

Don't be overawed by the achievements of others
Follow and learn
And make your own dreams come true.

Don't Fix It

Sometimes you just have to roll with the punches
And go with the flow
Sometimes things are outside your control
Sometimes you have to just let it be

Not everything needs fixing
Sometimes it is time for renewal
Destiny may have plans for you
More than you care to imagine
More than you dare

So just observe and let it be.

Karma

Little deeds of kindness
A little time helping others
A little time to listen
A little time to give your time
A little of yours to share.
A little time spent in prayer
A little act of compassion
That is all you need
To achieve.

Send out thoughts of love into the world
For its energy will return
It is the law of Karma
It is the cosmic law.

TWISTS & TURNS

The twists and turns of life
And its ups and downs
Will bring you face to face
With many successes and failures

The best you can do
Is to do your best
Ride the ups & downs
And hope that some luck comes your way

And when it does
Don't mistake it for achievement
Don't fool yourself
You were never in charge.

FORGIVE YOURSELF

To be without error
Would be untrue
So, forgive yourself

You may win sometimes
And sometimes you may face defeat
You did your best
So, forgive yourself

The smartest of us can sometimes be fooled
You are only human
So, forgive yourself

Let the drama unfold
And return to yourself
As the curtain falls

Life is more than success and failure
It is honesty and kindness and friendship and love
So, forgive yourself

BROWN LEAVES

Brown leaves in Fall

Fallen and discarded

Away from their roots

And no longer green

Yet dancing in the wind

When it blows

Life will be a gentle breeze sometimes

And sometimes there will be storms

Be like the brown leaves and dance in the wind

When it blows.

OPINIONS

Opinions, opinions, be careful of opinions
We form strong opinions on weak information
We need good questions not opinions
We need acceptance not opinions
We need to nurture relationships not be limited by opinions
We need to learn to observe and to analyse
Before we risk forming an opinion
We need to learn to change our opinions in a changing world
But as you may be aware
It's easier to form an opinion than to change one.
Do we need opinions?

The Worry Habit

New worries have taken over my mind
Yesterday's concerns are fading away
Observe your thoughts
And allow them to fade away

For you are not your thoughts
Nor your imaginations
Look inwards to find your true self
And rise above the good and the bad
For they are mostly interchangeable
With the passage of time

Carry on with your efforts
Let patience, acceptance and gratitude be your tools
The rewards may or may not come
Make your efforts your reward
And allow for providence to come through

Mind Control

Let your brain serve you
Let it not fool you
The impressions of the world
Are mostly your imaginations
Let your mind know the real from unreal
Let your mind be in control

Knowledge is important
Wisdom is more
Knowledge tells you what you wish to know
Wisdom tells you how to use it
If knowledge is power
Wisdom is discretion
If knowledge is light
Wisdom is the switch

Knowledge can be acquired
Wisdom needs developing
So be knowledgeable
But be wise.

HEALTH

Every part of your body has its own consciousness
So, approach your body with genuine compassion
Communicate with the cells in your body
Your cells are listening

Close your eyes and go deep to reach yourself
And realise
The power of healing
May the thirty trillion cells in your body
Always dance with joy

Imposter

Each day I ask the man in the mirror
Who you really are, what do you want to be ?
I hear a strong whisper
You want to be yourself; you want to be free
I hurriedly get ready and go to work
Each day I ask the same question
I go to work
Another day lost
And life passes by.

BE GRATEFUL

When you wake up in the morning and the sun is shining, there's not a cloud in the sky and you are alive
Be grateful

When you wake up in the morning and its dark and cloudy and you are alive
Be grateful

When you feel a little low, count all your blessings in a row
You know growth happens when it pours
Be grateful

Eat less, chew more, take a walk in the park, thank the trees and all of nature; we are interdependent, you know
Be grateful

When you turn the tap on, and it flows
Be grateful

You will attract positive vibes when you acknowledge what you have
Be grateful

When you see a little child play with simple toys,
you see joy
Be the grown-up but don't lose the child
Be grateful

Every once in a while, in your busy lives, stop and
breathe in life, you are alive
Be grateful

When you are alive, so much is possible
Be grateful

WAR

I have been at war many times
With myself
Over-thinking, worry, anxiety and guilt
Have depleted my emotional reserves
It's time for compassion and self-realisation
It's time to make peace

Mind Influencers

Be aware of the places you visit

For places have energy

Be aware of the time of day

For each hour has its own purpose

Be aware of what you eat and drink

For it may alter your physical and mental wellbeing

Be aware of your past memories

For these can shape the person you are today

Be aware of your associations

For they can affect your success

Be aware, choose wisely

Be mindful of the influences in your life.

Simple Joys

The joy of achievement, the joy of success,
I have enjoyed these joys
But the joy of all joys, I found
Was the joy of walking with my daughter in the park

RESPECT

If you love your Mum and have a sister or a daughter
Then hey Guys, give a little respect
to the women of the world
The tears you cause could easily be yours
If it happened to your own
So, give a little respect to the women of the World.

The weak abuse
The strong protect
Control is only real
When it is self-control
So, give a little respect to the women of the World

Power is not force
Power is courage and tolerance
It is strength and acceptance
And it is love
So, give a little respect to the women of the World

Remember, you were born of a Woman
Your real source of power
Truly your other and equal half
So, give a little respect to the women of the World.

THE STRUGGLE

Life is a struggle
But I am still here
Still fighting

Struggles can mould you
And ground you
So, success won't spoil you
And failure won't drown you

Adjust your sight as you go through dark places
Sharpen your vision through the night
Await for dawn, for it will surely come
And you will appreciate the day again.

Life is a struggle
But I am still here
Still fighting.

A ROLLING STONE

A rolling stone gathers no moss
Why be still and covered in moss
Lonely on a hilltop
Roll down the hill
And rub off the rocks
Become rounded and smooth
Sail across the seas
To places afar
To become from a stone to a star

In Love in Vain

In vain I try to tell her that
I love her and will always do
In vain she tries to tell me that
Our love is still so young, so new

That time alone will tell and
Help to make her mind
But I know our love will stay
Young and fresh with the passage of time

So what good is time to me that
Keeps me away from her
She stops to think, she stops again

In vain, I try to tell her to
Come with me and
Be with me
Always.

Re-Invent Yourself

Whether you believe or don't believe in reincarnation
You don't have to die for it

Humility

Humility comes naturally to me
Life has been crowded with mistakes
There's hardly any space for arrogance or pride

Positive Vanity

Be vain, be vain
It can be good for you
Be vain, be vain
Look up to yourself
And not down on others

Imagine yourself slim
Imagine yourself rich
Imagine yourself in good health
Imagine yourself achieving
Whatever you wish to achieve

Bathe yourself in glory
Be proud but not in excess
Be nice to yourself and others
Feel the positive effects of vanity
And the resolve it brings

Be vain, be vain
It can be good for you

LOVE

Take time to hold hands

Take time to gaze into each other's eyes

Take time to spend time with each other

Take time to say the things you always meant to say

And mean the things you say

Do the things you always meant to do.

For regrets there will be many

As time slips by

Never to return

And there will be no more time

THE PURPOSE OF LIFE

Is there a need for one?
Just live it everyday
Find joy in everything

Break free from your cocoon
Set upon a journey of discovery
Discover me
Discover you

Discover Life

STRESS AND ADDICTION

Some seek solace in work
Some in food
Some in sex and drugs
And some in booze

Some gamble
Some buy stuff they don't need

And yet simply becoming aware
Can move the unconscious to the conscious
The beginning of a new mindset
Opening up options
To choose from

To form new habits or
No habits at all

EDUCATION RE-VISITED

I know that two and two equals four
And a triangle has three sides
I know four ways to calculate
The area of a circle

I know the names of all the continents
And the names of all the seas
And oceans

I can recite long poems
And read the classics
I speak several languages
Just like natives do

I know that lava flows from volcanoes
And the distance to the moon
I know the names of all the constellations
And all about space too

But I don't know much about everyday finance
Or the law for that matter
And not much about success and failure
Or how to overcome fear of risks.

I don't know much about confidence
Or how to rise up after a fall
I haven't learnt to navigate
The choppy waters of life

I don't know much about contentment
Or that co-operation is better than competition
That sharing is better than accumulation
And that kindness and charity
Can make you feel fulfilled

That winning is not everything
That the good of all can be very rewarding
I don't know how to still my mind
And search for my true self

We need to change the system

HOPE

A young man ends his life
Killed by his own thoughts
Thoughts of loneliness and no care
Thoughts of no hope and despair

All he needed was a little attention
Some encouragement
Someone to talk to
A little love and care

Have we become so insular
So absorbed in an unreal world
The virtual seems real and
The real unreal

Let us return to a place we used to know
A place to call our own
A place of safety
To nurture and to care

WHY OH WHY?

Why, oh Why, oh Why, oh Why?
I have asked myself a million times
But never did I get a reply

What can I do now, I asked myself once
And the replies came pouring in

If You Only Knew

If you only knew that most of your fears would not come true

If you only knew that sometimes when things happen, they turn out best for you

If you only knew that you have the power to face your fears and be in control once more

If you only knew that all things must pass, and nothing stays the same

If you only knew that there are ups and downs in every life and you can learn to rise again

If you only knew what your positive imagination could do for you

If you only knew that the good actions you perform are their own reward

If you only knew that the future could be yours if you wanted to

If you only knew that the simple joys of life could set you free

Would you fret and would you worry?

BODY LANGUAGE

Be the person you wish you want to be
Walk like the person you wish you want to be
Talk like the person you wish you want to be
Not with arrogance but with conviction
Like an actor performing

Your posture will impact your emotions,
Your self-confidence and your sense of relaxation
Your physiology will change your psychology
And alter your behaviour

So, walk tall and keep smiling
And surely you will reach your success.

ETERNITY

I may be gone
But I will still be there
In your words, your actions
And your smile

I may be gone
But I will still be there
In the gentle rain that feels
Like a father's kiss
On a daughter's forehead

I may be gone
But I will still be there
In your laughter, your happiness and
In your tears too

I may be gone
But I will still be there
In your positive attitude
Your self-confidence
And your courage

I may be gone
But I will still be there
In your past and present
And the future generations

I may be gone
But I will still be there
So, do not grieve
For I will walk with you
When you think of me

ACCIDENTS

True accidents rarely happen
Most harm is self-harm
Pull back your racing mind
Enjoy the moment

For the past is gone
And the future is not yours
And may never be

Immerse yourself in the present
For there is only the
Here and now.

JUST LIKE YOU

I am just like you
In spirit and mind
I have feelings just like you have
I have urges, desires, ambitions, hopes & dreams
Just like you have

I want to make a difference
To share & contribute
To society
To reach my potential
Just like you do

I am wheelchair bound
Not bound to my wheelchair
I have got over my disability
But I am struggling daily with the attitude to
disability

I may be mobile
But I want to feel free

THE PRISON

In a prison of my making
Surrounded by imaginary iron bars
With an unlocked door
And no guards to watch over
Struggling to be free

PEACE OF MIND

Lost in the desert
Losing my mind
Looking for my oasis
In the maelstrom of my mind

I see an oasis
But it's just a mirage
I close my eyes and banish all thoughts
The storm in my mind slowly subsides
I open my eyes
I have found my oasis.

ARTHUR

Arthur passed away quietly in his flat last night
The TV still on and a half-drunk cup
of cold tea by his side
He wasn't very old
Just looked older than his years

Some say his heart stopped
Some say it was broken

Arthur once had a life full of purpose
Of companionship and of conversations
Of work and fun and evenings out
Just like you and me.

Devoid of human contact
In recent times
On his own and no one to talk to
Had dimmed the twinkle in his eyes

With not much to look forward to
A life of loneliness and just existence
Arthur took his last sip of life and said goodbye.

So, if you happen to know of Arthur in your
neighbourhood
Do drop by to say Hello
You could just be saving a life
And in return
Pick up some wisdom
Gathered over the years.

NB: Isolation as risk factors for mortality. The stand out conclusion from this was that loneliness is likely to increase the risk of death by 26%.

HAVE A LAUGH

Have a laugh
You don't need a reason

Have a laugh
It will widen your arteries and
Increase your blood flow

Have a laugh
It will release those endorphins and
Boost your immune system

Have a laugh
It will lower your stress hormones and
Increase your T cells

Have a laugh
It will up the oxygen to your brain and
Improve your memory

Have a laugh
It will enhance your mood and
Increase your creativity

Have a laugh
It will exercise your muscles and
Keep you sane

You have several reasons to have a laugh. but
Do you need a reason to have a laugh?

Why bother with reasons
Just have a laugh

NB: The above is not medical advice

HAPPINESS POSTPONED

I'll be happy
When all this is sorted
And when all this is sorted
There'll be other things to sort out
And I'll be happy when they are sorted
When will all things be sorted
Who knows?

Epitaph

Life spent dreaming
So much potential
So little achieved